NOT TONIGHT DEAR, I HAVE A COMPUTER

By

STEVE SCARBOROUGH

CCC PUBLICATIONS

Published by
CCC Publications
9725 Lurline Avenue
Chatsworth, CA 91311

Manufactured in the United States of America

Cover ©1998 CCC Publications

Cover/Interior production by Klaus Selbrede

ISBN: 1-57644-069-9

If your local U.S. bookstore is out of stock, copies of this book may be obtained by mailing check or money order for $6.95 per book (plus $2.75 to cover postage and handling) to: CCC Publications; 9725 Lurline Avenue, Chatsworth, CA 91311

Pre-publication Edition – 9/98

INTRODUCTION

Does your heart beat faster when a friend talks about buying a new computer? Do you salivate when your office gets new software? Can't wait to turn on your computer in the morning? Do you find yourself at computer super store instead of the mall? Do you catch yourself fantasizing about going on-line the minute you're free from work? Do you walk around like a Tyrannosaurus Rex with your hands in a keyboard position?

Techie, newbie, nethead, Netniks, geeks, cyber-punks. No, just the vast group of computer owners who are excited by big hard drives and swollen RAM and who would grovel for a 1000x CD-ROM.

This book is about all the quirks and peculiarities that characterize people who are obsessed with their computers. Cyberplebes. How do you know if you have become a little over-infatuated with your PC?

OR...

You get e-mail telling you that dinner is ready.

1

Your kids only recognize
you by the back of
your head

Your new computer
costs more than
your Lexus

Your heart races while you drive home from work as you plan your evening on the computer

You can sit at your PC all day long and do absolutely, entirely nothing

You hire a nanny to watch your children so you can *surf* all day without interruption

Your phone bill is more than your house payment

You refer to things as
being offline or online

Like Time is an offline
magazine - while Slate is
the online mag

Or the Metropolitan is an
offline museum — because
you surf to art.com

And Disneyland is an
offline amusement park

You hover around the installer every time a new computer arrives at the office

Your keyboard is padded in case you nod off

Your freezer is packed
solid with finger food
and quick-snacks

You have more computer
games than your kids
have toys

When you sign on in a chat room everyone says "Norm!"

You e-mail your husband instructions on how to make dinner - "set oven at 350 . . ."

You can't fall asleep without the hum of your computer fan

Your favorite conversation opener is "Can you believe how cheap computers are these days?"

You have renamed your dog "Browser"

You visit the library just to do a computer search with no intention of checking out a book

You used AutoCAD to decide where to put your couch

You insist that your boyfriends get a virus check

You use voice recognition software to talk to your kids

On average you wear out three mouses per month

You are actually excited AOL is busy just so you can keep clicking the *sign on* button a hundred times

You let your Time & Newsweek subs expire to subscribe to Website, Wired, and The Net magazines

You steal your kids' MegaPet so that you can have a computer chip in your pocket

Not counting your monitor, the only TV you watch anymore is CNET – the cable Web Show

You introduce
your spouse as
*TheWife@
myhome.com*

When your computer
gets a virus and you
develop symptoms too

You skip an appointment with the hairdresser to redesign your screensaver

Your idea of a hot fantasy is being a computer game developer for Westwood Studios

Your husband doesn't know it but, you drop all your laundry at the cleaners to spend more time on the computer

JAVA no longer means coffee but "motion"

The hot Friday night dates you brag about are really in the "desperate" chat room

The only time you see the outside world is through the ferret cam or volcano cam

The method you use to decide if you need an umbrella is to check *weather.com*

Your honeymoon suite had duel terminals with a network across the bed

You volunteer to make the T-shirts for your daughter's soccer league so you can use your new color printer

You printed out all 3,000 of your graphic files just to see how they would look on paper

Your nightly greeting, "What's for dinner, Dear?" is met by a computer printout

When you have reached the depths of despair your first thought is to surf to *www.dependence@ support.com* for help

Your e-mail signature is "My name is Bill and I am an online addict"

If it were not for the "party on down" room on IRC Chat you would have no social life at all

Soccer mom has
changed into
computer mom

You insist that your
spouse drive (on trips) so
you can compute on
your laptop

You sneak down to the computer lab on Saturday nights

You spend your time on the Usenet groups downloading the latest JPEG's of cows and duck decoys

Your idea of listening to great jazzy sounds is through your monitor speaker at *musicology.com*

Colon Slash/Slash is your favorite grunge-punk rock group

You follow every play
of that pro sports game
at the web site instead
of on TV

You have upgraded so
much that you use
those little metal
slot covers for
garden stakes

You have a $4,000 CD home stereo system and you play music CDs on your $15 computer speakers

You keep losing weight but you don't want to stop computing to eat

You transfer your software games from your organizer to your palmtop to your laptop to your desktop to your server, just so you will never be without them

Your spouse has to trick you into leaving your computer desk (by telling you a store has free software) just to clean out the crumbs from your chair and disinfect your area

You order-in Chinese so you can continue cataloging all your recipes on disk

You prolong getting your college degree just so you can have free access to the all those PCs in the computer lab

You are on your third
color cartridge . . .
this week

After a hard day at
work, giving online
support, you relax by
setting up an Excel
worksheet for the tools
stored in your garage

You wake up worried about the people in your Simm City

The light on your VCR is still flashing "12:00," but you don't care – you'd rather run your virus program one more time

You put your make-up
on using the reflection
in the monitor

Your family and friends
call you by your
user name

You think an acceptable excuse for being late for work is checking your e-mail

You relate everything in your life in terms of AC & BC (After Computer & Before Computer)

Every conversation at a party starts with "Ain't it great how cheap RAM is?"

When you talk you unconsciously tap your fingers on the desk in time with your words

You have your own set
of keys to the college
computer lab

SPF 2000 is not enough
for you when you
go outside

You have your own
virtual mug at the
HyperDrive coffee house

You are more impressed
with clip art than works
by the Masters

Vegging out in front of
the TV has turned into
vegging out in front of
the computer

When your husband said he was bringing something electric to bed you hoped he meant a laptop

You know what :-} is and know how to create it with your keyboard

When you sit in a chair,
you automatically hold
your arms out like a
kangaroo

Sexy talk is hearing your
date describe his hard-
ware system component
by component

You have computer
Post-it notes stuck
around on the inside of
your monitor screen

Your idea of keeping up
with the latest in contem-
porary literature is
reading Wasting Time
with Windows

When you give a party
you spend so much time
with PC Bartender you
never actually mix
a drink

After work, you turn the
switch on your PC before
popping open a beer

All your relatives'
computers used to
be yours

Your kids are using your
last computer as a
Barbie playhouse

Archaeology to you is digging through the back room of We Fix Computers at Wholesale

Your spouse says, "Not tonight honey," and you say, "Okay, no problem, I'll just bang away on my computer for a while."

The only time you really mediate is at *Yoga.com*

Your pet macaw says "need more RAM!"

Your new pick-up line in bars is, "So, do you compute often?"

You have never actually physically held the little dog or the top hat while playing monopoly

You hold funerals for users who get kicked off AOL

You don't know how much a postage stamp costs these days

You are trying to scrape up enough money to start a computer business on the side just to be able to support your upgrade habit

On Sunday mornings you wake up early and get dressed to attend services at *McChurch@ Tabernacle.com*

The most tactile you get is caressing those little raised dots on the keyboard

Your photo album is digital

You can describe the avatar people in your chat group better than your own family

Your online service calls YOU for support

You go online to look up
the spelling of common
words at *dictionary.com*

You would spend any
amount of money to trim
download times

Everyone you know has
you design computer
Xmas cards for them

You had to get another hard drive just for your clipart

You compulsively click on all the hyperlinks at every web site you visit

You know that a cookie is an Internet identifier sent to your PC

Your wife is dropping
hints about a
NetMeeting at
Therapist.com

You have one of those
combat joysticks that
looks like it was
designed by Geiger

You abbreviate all
your words down
to eight letters

. . . and add a three-
letter extension like,
"Then the conversa with
software support
terminat and I hung up
the telephon and went to
bed.com"

When you say, "let's do lunch" you mean meet at *Theplace.com* with your comic persona

In your junk drawer, next to your old wrist watches, is a pile of used mouses

You have never even
seen a typewriter

You feel guilty for
spending too much time
with your work computer
and just know your
home computer is
getting jealous

You carry an extra mouse around in your fannypack

Your idea of bringing a sexy toy to bed is a natural shaped keyboard

You met your spouse
online

You have gone online as
a PHD from Harvard,
who flies your own jet
around to compete in
body builder contests
when you aren't
modeling for GQ

The only reason you fixed the roof leak is because it started to drip onto your keyboard

You surf to *Playboy.com* just to read the articles

You know how to write html

You pretend to be a salesman at Computer World and answer customer's questions just for fun

Your phone number is now your "voice number"

You put your kid's e-mail address on his underwear before sending him off to summer camp

You watch your rental movies from Blockbuster in the little window on your computer while playing Mist

You lie on the beach in Bermuda and read a computer manual

You moved the kids training toilet into your computer room
(for your own use)

Your child's first words are "more RAM"

At all times you carry
a set of those teeny tiny
screwdrivers in your
shirt pocket

Before your first date you
asked Dad for the keys
to the family computer

You feel cheated when the next generation of processor chip is released and trade up immediately

Your have your five-room house set up with an LAN Intranet network

You run NT - at home

Your biggest ambition in life is to set the world record for surfing through the most WWW sites in one 24-hour period

Your favorite song is on a wav. file

Instead of mowing, you run out and spray your yard with grass killer to free up more weekend computer time

You take your laptop to your son's Bar Mitzvah

You set up video confer-
encing on your kids'
computer so you could
see what they look like

Cyber Discounts Inc. has
an offsite warehouse in
your garage

To you, "gourmet" is
Deluxe Hot Pockets

You think the joke about
Bill Gates and the rubber
chicken is funny

You named your kids
Gates, Eudora and
Dotcom

You can dissemble and reassemble your computer case blindfolded – with one hand tied behind your back

Your only checkbook record is in Quickbooks

Your coffee maker, your
toaster and your vacuum
are ancient coughing
wrecks but your latest
PC is only 2 weeks old

You have more "friends"
on your e-mail list than
your Xmas card list

You can remember all your passwords but forget your wedding anniversary

You have one of those wristwatches that uploads your schedule from your computer

You are compelled to stop and check your e-mail at the airport computer kiosk

You are the one who sneaks into your laptop computer during take-offs and landings

Your laptop costs more than your last family vacation - three weeks at Euro Disney

You wake up at 4 am to get a drink of water and check your e-mail on the way back to bed

You used to bake the kids cookies, now you only build on Internet "cookies"

You get a tattoo that has your sweetheart's e-mail address

You laugh out loud when someone mentions their 9600 baud modem on their 486

You have considered selling a body part to get more computer stuff

You get physical withdrawals within five minutes after turning off your computer

You won't be satisfied until you have a 94x CD-ROM

You have come close to
assaulting some
unsuspecting newbie
just for saying,
"information
super highway"

You bought a gross of straws so you don't have to take your hands from the keyboard

You have ever, crazily, said, "Buy what you want Dear, I just found a great site"

You volunteer to be a "shill" at ComputerLand and brag about computers to potential customers

You have enough old ram chips to melt down and use the gold for an engagement ring

Your house is so computerized you can flush all your toilets with one touch of your keyboard

You moved your TV lounger into the computer room

You lost the case cover to your computer

A homeless person would drool over the crumbs in your keyboard

You back up your hard drives every three minutes

You have keyboard indentations in your forehead from falling asleep at your PC

You were late for your wedding because you had to finish reading your e-mail

You don't know that
CDs are also an
investment

Your butt is as
flat as your
computer screen

You have more screen
savers than minutes
in the day

You can instantly recall
AOL's phone number
but have to look up
your own

You can mimic the
connection noises a
modem makes

You turn on your computer before your morning coffee

You moved your computer into the bedroom and installed a mirror on the ceiling over it

BC - you were described as the strong silent type, AC - you're just the silent type sitting at the computer

Your kids explain to their class that your job is working at the computer at home

Your magazine rack in the bathroom has a laptop

You have a great handicap in software Links but you don't even own a golf club

You have a mouse pad for every mood

Your tombstone will read
dead.com

Your family calls you on
the cell phone that sits by
your PC

You had "QWERTY
uiop" tattooed on the
back of your fingers

When you are asked for
your home address you
absent-mindedly give
your e-mail address

You think a microwave
pizza takes too long
to cook

You resist sitting down at your computer till after dinner just to hear your wife sarcastically say "See you in the morning"

To you, faxes are obsolete

A relative complains the phone is busy, and you lie about having absent-mindedly left it off the hook

It's been only two hours since you last checked your e-mail

Your neighbor's teens are referred to as juvenile delinquents, punks and hoodlums – but your kids are webheads, netnicks and Cyberplebes

You feel it is an insult to read an instruction manual or even "Getting Started"

You use all your allotted sick days to stay home and surf the Web

On vacation you sneak away to use the ATM just to get in some computer time

You rationalize that working the mouse is exercise

You know the secret programmer's trick for 'god mode' in Wolf's Island 3-D

All your T-shirts and baseball caps have computer logos

It is a warm beautiful Summer afternoon and you can't wait to turn on your computer

At the reading of your will, all your heirs will hear which computer they'll get

Your business cards
display your e-mail
address ABOVE
your name

You sit and stare for
hours at your inbox
waiting for new e-mail

You invite friends over
for a wild game of
computer jeopardy

You have your own
coffee mug in the
Computer City
break room

Your idea of exercise is rolling your chair back and forth between your computers

Every calendar in your house was made on your PC

You pull up the street maps of exotic distant cities on Digimap, not because you are going there - but just because it's fun

The thought of a computer virus scares you more than AIDS

You watch TV with closed captioning on because it's like being in a chat room

You have weekly yard sales with just your old computer stuff

You wear a brace for carpal tunnel syndrome, and still spend hours at the keyboard

You have a room full of encyclopedias but you still pop in that CD-ROM to look up "giraffes"

You find yourself
begging your friends to
go online so you can
hangout and talk

You upgrade your
eyeglass prescription -
twice a month

Your vanity plates refer to your e-mail address

You rent a laptop and take it with you to the hospital to use while waiting for the operation

Your boyfriend e-mails you a goodnight (-:~ after a date

You up and moved your family just to be near Intel HQ

You gave up smoking
cold turkey the day you
heard it was harmful to
computer parts

u cn read tis

You've ever given one of those chocolate computer disks as a gift

Given the choice, you like turning on your computer more than your spouse

You considered yourself a virgin before your first computer

At first you left the vacuum out to pretend like you were still cleaning but then you had to break down and get a maid

You have created
a separate bank
account for your ISP
bills

You find out your spouse
is divorcing you only
when a lawyer serves
you via e-mail

The maid dusts you along with the furniture

You use the baby monitor to listen for "You have mail!"

You get arrested and for
your one phone call
you ask for a PC
and a modem

You keep a grand
running total of how
many e-mails you have
ever received

You have never met
your best friend,
face to face

You once introduced
your spouse as your
"service provider"

You put on special mood
music before going into
one of those chat rooms

You tell people that your
blood shot eyes are from
a hard night drinking
and partying

You finally got smart and bought stock in eye wash companies

You refuse to accept a promotion to a department that does not have computers on everyone's desk

Your last date
consisted of going to
PinkLobster.com and
then to the
Moviesplex.com

You had your account
cancelled for over-using
your "unlimited" account

Your online time is
measured not with a
clock but with a calendar

You find yourself using
your whole lunch
break playing
Zoom Attack 3-D

You make up excuses to stay late and finish playing games that you started at lunch

You panic when you learn that there is no computer at your vacation spot

You e-mail yourself from AOL to CompuServe, just to get mail

You always ask for a table near outlets at restaurants, so you can plug in your laptop

You have a great tan,
not from the sun,
but from the monitor
screen radiation

Your home vacation
movies consist of video
captures from the Web
sites you have visited

Your kids use their
Popsicle money to
put your picture on
a milk carton

You grunt out a sensual
moan every time a new
window opens

Your idea of camping out is taking an ice chest full of beer and sandwiches into the computer room

You worked hard for 15 years climbing the corporate ladder, getting that corner office on the top floor overlooking the bay – just to spend all your time glued to your computer screen

Your wife gave a house tour to new friends and she blurted out, "Pay no attention to the man behind the monitor!"

You and your husband
are both high paid
executives and the main
dispute in your divorce
is who gets custody
of the computer

You are in such a hurry
to get back to your
computer you don't
even ask for a
goodnight kiss

You have your alarm set
at regular intervals
during the night so you
can check your e-mail

You carry a picture
of your computer
in your wallet.

TITLES BY CCC PUBLICATIONS

Blank Books ($3.99)
SEX AFTER BABY
SEX AFTER 30
SEX AFTER 40
SEX AFTER 50

Retail $4.95 – $4.99
30 – DEAL WITH IT!
40 – DEAL WITH IT!
50 – DEAL WITH IT!
60 – DEAL WITH IT!
RETIRED – DEAL WITH IT!
"?" book
POSITIVELY PREGNANT
CAN SEX IMPROVE YOUR GOLF?
THE COMPLETE BOOGER BOOK
FLYING FUNNIES
MARITAL BLISS & OXYMORONS
THE DEFINITIVE FART BOOK
THE COMPLETE WIMP'S GUIDE TO SEX
THE VERY VERY SEXY ADULT DOT-TO-DOT BOOK
THE CAT OWNER'S SHAPE UP MANUAL
THE OFFICE FROM HELL
FITNESS FANATICS
YOUNGER MEN ARE BETTER THAN RETIN-A
BUT OSSIFER, IT'S NOT MY FAULT
YOU KNOW YOU'RE AN OLD FART WHEN...
1001 WAYS TO PROCRASTINATE
HORMONES FROM HELL II
SHARING THE ROAD WITH IDIOTS
THE GREATEST ANSWERING MACHINE MESSAGES
WHAT DO WE DO NOW??
HOW TO TALK YOU WAY OUT OF A TRAFFIC TICKET
THE BOTTOM HALF
LIFE'S MOST EMBARRASSING MOMENTS
HOW TO ENTERTAIN PEOPLE YOU HATE

YOUR GUIDE TO CORPORATE SURVIVAL
THE SUPERIOR PERSON'S GUIDE
GIFTING RIGHT
NO HANG-UPS (Volumes I, II & III – $3.95 ea.)
TOTALLY OUTRAGEOUS BUMPER-SNICKERS ($2.95)

Retail $5.95
SINGLE WOMEN VS. MARRIED WOMEN
TAKE A WOMAN'S WORD FOR IT
SEXY CROTCHWORD PUZZLES
SO, YOU'RE GETTING MARRIED
YOU KNOW HE'S A WOMANIZING SLIMEBALL WHEN...
GETTING OLD SUCKS
WHY GOD MAKES BALD GUYS
OH BABY!
PMS CRAZED: TOUCH ME AND I'LL KILL YOU!
OVER THE HILL – DEAL WITH IT!
WHY MEN ARE CLUELESS
THE BOOK OF WHITE TRASH
THE ART OF MOONING
GOLFAHOLICS
CRINKLED 'N' WRINKLED
SMART COMEBACKS FOR STUPID QUESTIONS
YIKES! IT'S ANOTHER BIRTHDAY
SEX IS A GAME
SEX AND YOUR STARS
SIGNS YOUR SEX LIFE IS DEAD
40 AND HOLDING YOUR OWN
50 AND HOLDING YOUR OWN
MALE BASHING: WOMEN'S FAVORITE PAS-TIME
THINGS YOU CAN DO WITH A USELESS MAN
MORE THINGS YOU CAN DO WITH A USELESS MAN
RETIREMENT: THE GET EVEN YEARS
THE WORLD'S GREATEST PUT-DOWN LINES
LITTLE INSTRUCTION BOOK OF THE RICH & FAMOUS